W9-ARR-063

Family Business Compensation

Craig E. Aronoff, Ph.D. and
John L. Ward, Ph.D.

Family Business Leadership Series, No. 5

Family Enterprise Publishers
P.O. Box 4356
Marietta, GA 30061-4356

ISSN: 1071-5010
ISBN: 0-9651011-5-0
© 1993
Fourth Printing

Family Business Leadership Series

We believe that family businesses are special, not only to the families that own and manage them but to our society and to the private enterprise system. Having worked and interacted with hundreds of family enterprises in the past twenty years, we offer the insights of that experience and the collected wisdom of the world's best and most successful family firms.

This volume is a part of a series offering practical guidance for family businesses seeking to manage the special challenges and opportunities confronting them.

To order additional copies, contact:
Family Enterprise Publishers
1220-B Kennestone Circle
Marietta, Georgia 30066
Tel: 1-800-551-0633
Web Sites: www.efamilybusiness.com
www.arthurandersen.com

Quantity discounts are available.

Other volumes in the series include:

Family Business Succession: The Final Test of Greatness

Family Meetings: How to Build a Stronger Family and a Stronger Business

Another Kind of Hero: Preparing Successors For Leadership

How Families Work Together

Family Business Compensation

How to Choose & Use Advisors: Getting the Best Professional Family Business Advice

Financing Transitions: Managing Capital and Liquidity in the Family Business

Family Business Governance: Maximizing Family and Business Potential

Preparing Your Family Business For Strategic Change

Making Sibling Teams Work: The Next Generation

Developing Family Business Policies: Your Guide to the Future

Family Business Values: How to Assure a Legacy of Continuity and Success

More Than Family: Non-Family Executives in the Family Business

Contents

Tables and Exhibits

I. *Introduction*

Asked how they were paid, four members of the Smith family, all managers in the family business, answered with some pride, "We all receive the market rate. We pay the job, not the person."

Upon further questioning, one son revealed that he made $80,000, compared with $40,000 earned by others doing the same job. His father rushed to explain: "He does a good job. And he owns the business, after all. He's part of the family."

The second son, it seemed, had just received a midyear raise. On what basis? His wife had given birth and decided to quit her job for full-time motherhood. "We wanted to make up for the lost income," the father said.

The third second-generation manager, a daughter, had received a raise at the same time. The reason? The two younger siblings were close in age and had always been competitive with each other, so their father felt they should be paid equally. That meant that when the son got a raise, the daughter got the same amount.

■

Compensation is at the heart of more family-business questions than any other topic except succession. "What's fair pay among family members? How do I determine the appropriate pay for my son's job? How should shareholders in the business be paid? How can I resolve family disputes over pay and still have time to run the company?" All are common queries.

Pay is an immediate and tangible symbol of the family business's multifaceted relationship with the family members and others it employs. Unfortunately, cases like the Smiths' (a composite of examples from real family businesses) are all too common. **It is extremely easy to confuse a paycheck in the family business with return on ownership, parental concern, or methods of achieving emotional goals.** (Please see Exhibit 1.) The result is a mixed message that can damage the business and the family. With seemingly simple decisions about pay, the Smiths are actually undermining the credibility of their own stated business principles. By their actions, they are saying that rules on "paying the job" have no bearing on family members and that family members' personal needs override job contribution as a determinant of pay. No wonder compensation poses some of the most sensitive and complex problems family businesses face.

1

EXHIBIT 1

The Flow of Funds in a Family Business

ROLE CONFUSION

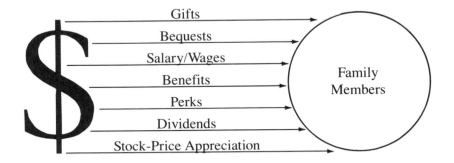

A RATIONAL SYSTEM

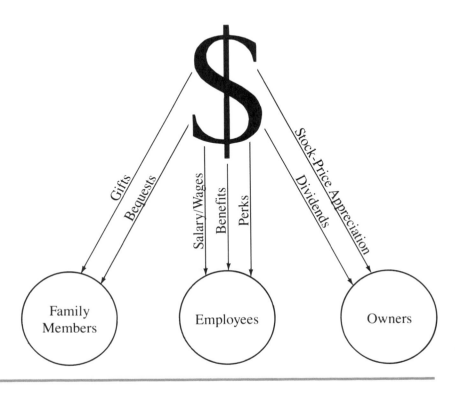

The importance of family business compensation planning is growing as more business owners bring multiple heirs into management. As discussed in No. 1 of **The Family Business Leadership Series**, *Family Business Succession: The Final Test of Greatness*, our studies show that family-business employment of multiple offspring is about twice as prevalent as it was even 10 to 15 years ago. Questions over how to pay family members; how to distinguish among their roles as employees, shareholders and loved ones; and how to maintain control over pay while keeping everyone happy, are driving many business owners to the brink of burnout.

No family business is immune to such tensions and misunderstandings. In one case, a younger brother who held a middle management job in the family business was offended by the higher salaries of an older sister and brother-in-law who had executive jobs, so he ran to the library to conduct some misguided research of his own in an effort to prove that he should make as much as they. The resulting discord blocked important planning for months.

In another case, a second-generation shareholder not active in the fast-growing family business complained about his siblings' big salaries, company cars and country club memberships. He disregarded the fact that in addition to paying him and other shareholders ample dividends, his siblings had tripled the size of the company, multiplied the value of his holdings and used the perks mostly on company business.

In another common problem, the details of employee compensation issues can mount to overwhelming levels in a growing business, engulfing the entrepreneur in minutia. As business owners spend more and more time on individual compensation questions, most at some point throw up their hands and say, "This pay and benefits business is crazy! We've got to have a system that makes all this make sense. We need some rational basis for these decisions — not all this stuff about people's emotions and personal needs!"

The more systematic compensation policies that result are aimed at encouraging professional growth among family members and other employees, as well as strategic accomplishment in the business. This means communicating a clear understanding of the value of various company jobs. It means weighing family members' expectations about lifestyle and, often, encouraging them to accept financial responsibility for themselves. It also means grasping a powerful tool to educate employees about the business, foster their trust and motivate them to perform well.

To accomplish this, many family businesses find they must discard some extremely common and popular notions about using pay for other purposes — ideas that can seriously hamper sound planning. Some of these notions, including several affecting the Smiths, are summarized in Table 1 and are examined in greater depth in **Section V** of this booklet.

In **Section II**, this booklet will explore some principles in developing a philosophy of compensation and some steps to follow in setting up a rational compensation plan. **Section III** offers ideas to help shape the expectations of family members and others around the ideals and goals that underlie sound pay practices. **Section IV** offers practical guidance on special issues such as the role of compensation in providing support for retiring business owners, compensation for nonfamily executives, and the use of compensation consultants. And **Section V** describes ways to build trust in the compensation system among family members, employees and other constituencies.

TABLE 1

TEN COMMON CAUSES OF
FAMILY BUSINESS PAY PROBLEMS

Role Confusion: Confusing payouts to family members in their roles as owners or loved ones with compensation for performing a job in the business.

Using Pay to Achieve Tax Savings: Using high salaries, perks or "phantom jobs" to transfer tax-deductible wealth to family members and avoid the heavy taxes imposed on dividends or gifts.

Using Pay to Maintain Parental Control: Using paychecks to convey messages or accomplish goals that have nothing to do with the market value of the job performed, such as luring reluctant children to work in the business or pressuring offspring to learn the importance of frugality.

Using Pay to Resolve Emotional Issues: Providing extra pay to ease uncomfortable feelings, such as parental guilt or resentment among offspring.

Preserving Secrecy at All Costs: Assuming that it is always indiscreet, impolite or just plain wrong to talk about how people working in the business are paid.

Confusing Business and Personal Funds: Assuming you can draw as much compensation from the business for as long as you need it to support the retirement lifestyle of your choice.

Taking Relationships for Granted: Assuming family members will trust, respect and be satisfied with your pay decisions just because they are family members.

Using Salary Substitutes: Offering titles, perks or other "salary substitutes" to appease family members unhappy with their pay.

Paying Everyone Too Little — or Too Much: Holding down top-management pay as a way of suppressing compensation throughout the organization; or, conversely, raising pay too high to retain people and avoid having to tell longtime employees how they are doing.

Using Pay to Smooth Ups and Downs: Altering pay to soften the impact on employees of ups and downs in the business, paying more in lean times to prove that you are a great boss and paying less in good times because there is no need to prove anything then.

II. *Steps in Building a Compensation Plan*

For many business owners, recognition of the need for change in compensation practices begins a process of transformation.

As they try to develop some kind of system, most family businesses create a philosophy of compensation and a way of communicating it to employees. In the process, compensation becomes a tool for carving out new milestones.

That's not to say that the business owner must embrace a rigid, bureaucratic method that eliminates human judgment or an owner's prerogative. No foolproof compensation formula exists. And no one wants a compensation system that has employees consulting a graph or pushing a button on a computer to find out what they will be paid next year. Rather, business owners at this stage, often with the help of directors or professional advisors, focus on systematically aligning compensation with their goals and mission for the business.

This section outlines the steps in building a rational compensation plan, from developing a philosophy of compensation, to building a framework for base pay and incentives, to communicating the plan to all concerned. Each family-business compensation plan can be tailored to the special values, goals and needs of the particular family firm. Yet the process outlined in Table 2 is similar to that used by many family businesses in developing a more systematic approach to compensation.

Developing a Philosophy of Compensation

A good compensation plan should keep everybody involved in the business working for what is best for all. To accomplish that, the plan must reflect the business's core philosophy.

A philosophy of compensation is a summation of the values, goals and principles that guide all decisions about salary, benefits and perks. It provides a framework that relieves decisionmakers of the burden of developing each compensation package individually. Building and describing this framework can force business owners to assess their most fundamental goals.

A central question is how the company remains competitive. Some companies, for instance, stress increasing **shareholder value**. This emphasis on profit maximization may translate into hiring and retaining

TABLE 2

STEPS IN BUILDING A COMPENSATION PLAN

1. Decide on a philosophy of compensation, including whether to pay family members equal amounts or based on the market value of their jobs.

2. Determine the market value for particular jobs.

3. Consider whether you want pay to be set at the market average or whether you want to make a cultural statement with pay at levels above or below the market average.

4. Adjust pay to reflect qualitative characteristics of the job that make it more or less strategically important than one would assume based solely upon market value.

5. Decide if you also want to offer an annual incentive plan based on personal goals and/or company performance.

6. Negotiate personal goals and pay incentives for individuals and/or teams.

7. Establish classifications and criteria for assessing company performance.

8. Consider whether you want to have a long-term incentive plan.

9. If so, establish the criteria (i.e., book value increases) and classifications (i.e., increase book value 15 percent) for long-term incentives.

10. Communicate clearly to everyone the philosophy of compensation and your plan to review and possibly refine it each year.

people at relatively low pay, charging customers higher prices and keeping supplier costs low, resulting in the best possible returns to shareholders.

Others take an employee-driven approach that focuses on creating the best possible **opportunities and environment for employees**. This reasoning holds that if employees are encouraged through attractive pay, benefits and perks to perform at their highest potential, stockholders, customers and other constituents will benefit from improved productivity, efficiency and quality.

Other businesses put **service to the customer** first on the list. This reasoning holds that if customers are attracted and retained through low-priced, high-quality products, the business will grow, creating new jobs for employees and higher returns for shareholders.

Most business owners would agree to some extent with all of these priorities. The question is usually one of emphasis — which of these goals do strategists stress most often, and which are the most central to their mission? The answer can strongly influence how compensation philosophy is determined and articulated.

Another central issue is determining how jobs are valued. The backbone of compensation policy might be, for instance, that everyone is paid according to the market value of the job performed. Other family businesses may add "qualitative" criteria, such as the leadership, communication or analytical abilities required to do a particular job well in a particular company. Still others may decide to pay family members equally, reflecting their shared ownership interest.

Whatever the choices made on these issues, the fundamental requirement is that the compensation philosophy provide for a consistent, above-board approach to pay.

Should We Embrace a "Market" Approach? To avoid problems, there is no substitute for paying people based on the size and difficulty of the job, in relation to comparable jobs at comparable companies — and making sure that everyone understands that the marketplace provides the basis for the policy.

Market value is a fair and consistent guide to setting pay, and it is relatively easy to explain to employees and shareholders. Simply put, a market value philosophy means you pay an employee what it would cost you to hire someone else to do the job. Its objective basis reduces the potential for misunderstanding and manipulation. It gives family members and other employees a realistic view of the value of their work. And it drains negative emotion from sensitive family interactions over pay.

Yet "pay people what their job is worth" is easier to say than do. Some family businesses decide for good reason not to embrace a market value approach, and any business considering doing so for the first time should stop to consider the ramifications.

In some businesses, pay has been set on non-market criteria for a long time. Some family members and other loyal employees may have been increasingly overpaid over the years. Family members who have been relatively underpaid may not see any reason to stir up the issue and hurt people's feelings. The status quo may be acceptable, and introducing market data or consultants' appraisals that expose inequities may only open unnecessary wounds.

Before taking even preliminary steps to seek data or make comparisons with other businesses, the following questions should be considered:

1. How has pay for family members been set in the past?

2. Are there important reasons to change to a "market value" approach?

3. If we do get objective data and it shows significant inequities, what will we do then?

These issues are especially important when the business is passing to a new generation of family members. During preparation for succession, members of the younger generation should meet to discuss the above questions and decide whether a change is needed.

The "market value" approach does have some advantages at this stage, at least until next-generation successors become substantial shareholders. If inequities in pay exist, they inevitably will come to light at some point as the next generation assumes leadership and ownership. If potential problems are not addressed early, they will be even more painful and difficult to resolve later. In most cases, by the time that the successor generation is established in its careers, family businesses decide pay should be based on the market value of jobs.

But before determining the market value for jobs held by family members, do consider and discuss what steps you want to take if market value and actual pay are very different — either higher or lower. A little preparation will make family members less likely to respond defensively or mount an attack once comparable pay data is received. They also will have an opportunity to provide hands-on job descriptions to assist data-gatherers, and may learn something about their own jobs in the process.

Some examples of family-business compensation philosophies based on the market value of jobs follow in Exhibits 2 and 3.

Paying Family Members Equally. Compensation in the family business can raise a dilemma fundamental to family life: How does one grapple with inequalities among family members in meting out resources?

As discussed earlier in this booklet, the first real question when a family business includes multiple siblings or close relationship groupings is **whether you really want to pay what the job is worth**. Some business

EXHIBIT 2 ████████████████████████████████████

A Family Business Compensation Philosophy

■ We will compare pay and performance levels with those of businesses we compete with directly.

■ Our goal is to provide total compensation between the median and 75th percentile of comparable groups.

■ We will emphasize performance-based incentives at the expense of base salary.

■ Base salary will be at or below the median level for comparable groups. Individual salaries will be held within 20 percent of the midpoint for our comparison groups' salary range.

■ Annual incentives will exceed those of comparably sized competitors.

■ Long-term incentives will be based on results that add shareholder value.

An example under this philosophy of the compensation potential of one job: *Base salary is set at the median level for comparable groups of $136,000. The maximum base salary is $163,000 (median plus 20 percent) or a minimum of $109,000 (median minus 20 percent). The target for the short-term incentive in this job is 25 percent of compensation, or $34,000. The maximum short-term incentive is $68,000, or 50 percent of target. The target long-term incentive also is 25 percent of compensation, or $34,000. The maximum long-term incentive is $51,000, or 150 percent of target.*

---

owners will argue that all brothers and sisters should be paid equally — especially if they are equal stockholders. After all, these owners reason, aren't their stakes in the business worth more than any differences in job value? The shared risks and rewards of ownership may dwarf any concern about pay differences among individual jobs in the business. For instance, if each sibling owns 25 percent of a business valued at $10 million, a 10 percent increase or decrease in shareholder value means that each partner experiences a gain or loss of $250,000. Under this philosophy, compensation becomes a tool to develop family members into a team of equal or nearly equal business partners and co-managers.

EXHIBIT 3 ███████████████████████████████

The Compensation Philosophy of a Large Family Business with Inactive Shareholders

Here are some principles from the compensation philosophy of a large, second-generation family business with several family members who own stock but do not work in the company:

■ Compensation should be *objectively determined* relative to the real market value of comparable jobs;

■ Pay should be *somewhat conservative* given family ownership and the uncertainty of the economy.

■ Compensation should be at the median or midpoint of rewards for "target" performance at comparable companies, even though our targets (in some years, 15 percent ROE and 15 percent sales growth) are far higher than average.

■ Our salaries and short- and long-term bonus packages should compare with professionally-managed, public companies.

■ Pay is based on the "size of the job" (i.e., its complexity) — not the title.

■ For family executives, we tie long-term bonuses to shareholder value increases, as measured by a three-year average of our performance on growth and return on equity. Executives may take their long-term incentive in stock or cash, but they are encouraged by a 10 percent discount on stock prices to use this bonus to buy stock.

Under one model, siblings might all become members of an executive committee as the older generation begins transferring management authority. Each sibling might be paid, say, $50,000 a year for serving on the executive committee or team, regardless of his or her base pay. This equal reimbursement for sharing the policymaking role sends a strong message that leadership is carried jointly. It also conveys the importance of the role, making each sibling a "fraction of a president" in addition to his or her day-to-day responsibilities.

Another approach is to establish a team with a designated leader. This sets apart one member of the team as a CEO or president. Under this

EXHIBIT 4 ▰▰▰▰▰▰▰▰▰▰▰▰▰▰▰▰▰▰▰▰▰▰▰▰▰

An "Equal-Income" Compensation Philosophy for Sibling Partners in a Second-Generation Family Business

- Our long-range goal is "equal wealth" rather than "equal income," because all share equally in equity.

- Over time, our hope is that each will contribute substantially to the wealth of all.

- We will share new investment opportunities with each other, giving each a chance to participate.

- We want to ensure each adequate income from family resources to meet accustomed lifestyles. To that end, we will guarantee a minimum family income of $130,000.

- To reflect the high value and shared responsibility we assign to the executive committee function, an additional $40,000 will be paid each family member for serving on the executive committee.

- In addition to minimum family income, we want to offer each sibling pay reflecting the value of their job in the business.

- When desirable, we will offer some family members additional bonus opportunities on the job, if we believe it will increase the value of our shared business investment.

---

model, siblings are paid equally, but one person takes final responsibility for decisionmaking and tie-breaking if necessary. The CEO would receive additional compensation, perhaps $35,000 a year. The amount of extra pay should not be enormous, but it should be enough to reflect a meaningful responsibility rather than a token title.

Other businesses may base family members' paychecks on the market value of the jobs they perform, but they also want all to enjoy a certain minimum income to sustain comparable lifestyles. So they guarantee a "minimum family income" to all. In the example shown in Exhibit 4, a guaranteed minimum family income was established. A job salary based on the market value of each family member's position in the business was added to that, and an opportunity for additional merit bonuses was afforded family members in key positions. An advantage of such an approach is that money received by employees because of their roles as family members is clearly identified as such, and doesn't send mixed messages about the value of the job they perform in the business.

How the Culture of the Business May Affect Your Philosophy. Some business owners find compensation issues surprisingly difficult to deal with.

One reason is that any business's compensation policy is deeply rooted in its culture — the implicit beliefs, values, assumptions, habits and behavior patterns that color the fabric of the business. The reasons people are paid the way they are may be partly unconscious, and may arise from the personal and family history, and the deeply felt personal needs of the business leader or leaders. Any family business that tries to develop a philosophy of compensation may learn a great deal about itself in the process.

Let's take a look at how some kinds of family-business cultures can affect compensation.

The Entrepreneurial Culture. Many first-generation family businesses use compensation as a way to achieve tax savings and maximize the entrepreneur's control over the business. The entrepreneur has confidence in his or her ability to manage compensation on a case-by-case basis and maintains tight personal control over each individual's pay, perks, incentives, dividends and gifts. If a family member working in this kind of culture asks for a raise, the business owner may brush her off with, "Look at what we just did for you at Christmas! Let's not talk about compensation." Similarly, if a shareholder asks about returns on capital, the business owner may respond, "Remember what we did for you when you worked in the business? Let's not start talking about dividends." Secrecy and ambiguity about compensation keep power in the hands of the entrepreneur and prevent any complaints about fairness.

The Paternalistic or "Family-First" Culture. Decisions in this setting are guided by the business leader's judgment on how best to meet family needs. This leader might allot raises to children in financial trouble or offer hefty incentives to lure a young family member into the business, regardless of that person's merit or the job to be performed. The overriding concern in this setting is keeping the family together and working in harmony. The professional needs of individuals may be satisfied as long as they do not compromise the "family welfare," as interpreted by the

14

business leader. Maintaining secrecy about compensation is a likely component of this culture, because it increases the business leader's control over family relationships.

The Bureaucratic Culture. In this culture, the business owner creates such a rigid and complex process for setting compensation that any goals that might be achieved through managing pay are forgotten. Employees might all get the same percentage increases each year as part of a formalistic procedure, but no one's heart — or judgment — would be in the process. In such a system, compensation becomes an end and not a means. What people are paid has nothing to do with the direction or goals of the organization.

In some ways, a bureaucratic system is the opposite of an entrepreneurial culture. It sometimes even *results* from business-owner burnout *caused* by the pressures of the entrepreneurial culture. Some business owners become so pained by complex, subjective pay decisions that they create a bureaucratic system that completely removes decisionmaking from their shoulders. If a person complains about pay, the business owner then can shrug and say, "Look, I'm sorry, but you've been here 14 years in this job and that's what the pay level is." While this avoids the stress of the more personal entrepreneurial approach, it wastes the opportunity to make pay a strategic tool for family and business achievement.

The Custodial Culture. The overriding goal in this setting is to preserve shareholder value. Risk is minimized to conserve capital, and compensation and strategy tend to be conservative in an effort to maintain stable dividends. Some business owners in this culture underpay family members as a reminder that "everybody is here to serve the shareholders." This approach tips the balance sharply away from rewarding personal effort, and toward rewarding ownership. It gives family-member employees little incentive to work very hard. They may need to be reminded frequently that their rewards lie in the future, when their children inherit the shareholder value in the business that they are building now.

The Culture of Strategic Management. In this setting, **compensation is used as a tool to create a climate for achieving strategic goals and guiding the culture of the organization**. Pay might be based on performance, as measured against a set of objectives for each job that have been developed jointly by the employee and a key manager responsible for meeting strategic goals. This approach is based on a rational

TABLE 3 _____

SOME CRITERIA FOR DETERMINING A JOB'S MARKET VALUE

- Position (What are others in similar positions paid?)

- Industry

- Size of company

- Number of people supervised

- Dollar value of assets overseen

- Sales or revenue volume

- Cost of living, based on location

- Profitability

decisionmaking process. But it uses creative means to tie the compensation system to the unique strategic and cultural purposes of the organization.

Setting Base Pay in a Market-Value System

For businesses that decide to base compensation on a market-value philosophy, the next step is to determine the market value of jobs. Table 3 contains some criteria typically used in determining a job's market value.

To arrive at a reliable estimate of the market value of various jobs, most businesses gather data from comparable companies in comparable industries. If a compensation consultant is used, these experts can be expected not only to help evaluate jobs, but to explain to all involved what jobs are worth and why. The consultant should do a "blind" evaluation of jobs throughout the organization — that is, before you disclose current pay levels. That affords the opportunity to hear the consultant's assessment independent of any influence by current pay.

When the consultant compares your business's pay with others, find out what companies, industries or data bases are being used for comparison. Is the reference group regional or national? Public or private? Competitors or non-competitors? Another helpful step is to ask for pay data across the range for the comparison group, from the top 10 percent to the median to the bottom 10 percent, so you have a sense of the breadth of relevant pay practices.

An example of a typical layout of a base-pay market-value survey is contained in Table 4.

When this process is complete, the consultant may set a range of annual pay for each job, so that employees will know their salary potential as long as they stay in a certain post. If a job is deemed worth $22,000 to $28,000 a year, for example, an employee in that job will know that the top pay potential is $28,000, plus cost-of-living increases, for as long as he or she holds the position. That helps everyone involved understand that tenure alone is not enough to justify continual increases in compensation.

Other sources of information can be used as well. Some examples are contained in Table 5.

Relating Base Pay to the Market Average. The next step is to make a decision to pay at the market average, above the market average or below the market average. Each philosophy is defensible, but depends on clearly communicating the thinking.

Those who decide to pay "at the market average" may conclude that paying less is not fair, while paying more is throwing money away. They would add that individual departures from "market average" should only be made on special merit or on below-average preparation for the job.

Those who pay "above the market," such as at the 75th or 90th percentile, may be trying in that way to attract and retain above-average employees. They would say to their people, "We are looking for the best and expecting far better-than-average qualifications or performance from all."

Those who decide to pay "below the market" may argue that their business offers such extraordinary personal growth and development opportunities that "great people will come to work for us for reasons other than money." These business owners often believe that creating an above-average work environment is part of their mission. If people leave at an above-average rate, it's a valuable signal to top managers that the work environment is not as enriching as they may desire.

A decision about paying at, above or below the market average often is linked to the business's strategic plan. For example, an outside director of

TABLE 4

A Typical Layout of a Base Pay Market Value Survey*

Position	Region	REVENUES											
		$1-5m			$6-10m			$10-20m			>$20m		
		1st quartile	median	3rd quartile	1st quartile	median	3rd quartile	1st quartile	median	3rd quartile	1st quartile	median	3rd quartile
President/CEO	Northeast												
	South												
	Midwest												
	West												
VP Production	Northeast												
	South												
	Midwest												
	West												
Controller	Northeast												
	South												
	Midwest												
	West												
Etc.	Northeast												
	South												
	Midwest												
	West												

*Studies also frequently provide a table for incentive compensation and/or total of base and incentive compensation.

TABLE 5

SOME ADDED SOURCES OF COMPENSATION INFORMATION

1. *Business Week*. Annual survey in early May of CEO pay at hundreds of the biggest public companies, including the size of annual raises and comparisons of executives' total compensation to profitability, return on equity and shareholder returns. Also, features on linking pay to performance, incentive plans and other compensation issues.

2. *Forbes*. Annual rankings in late May of top-paid executives at 800 public companies, including gains in value of stock owned and five-year total compensation averages. Also, features on incentive pay, linking compensation to performance and other issues.

3. *Inc*. Occasional anonymous subscriber surveys showing average executive and employee pay, benefits and perks by region, industry and company size. Also, frequent articles and advice for smaller companies on compensation strategy.

4. Trade groups' pay surveys.

5. Local employer associations' regional salary surveys.

6. Regional business newspapers' salary surveys.

one successful, fast-growing family business knew the company had an ambitious strategic plan involving a five- to ten-year sales expansion to $250 million from $50 million currently. The company's management was crucial to that plan and brought a good deal of creative insight to bear on executing it.

"Shouldn't we be paying our top people at the 75th percentile?" the director asked. His reasoning: The top two or three people were hired to lead the company to $250 million. If the company is depending on them to do that, they should be paid as if the company were already there — or, at least, at the market average of a firm closer to that size. If they were paid the market average of a $50 million firm, they would surely be hired away by another firm with serious growth intentions.

Because the company hasn't attained its goal yet, of course, paying at the 75th percentile for a company of the current size may be a good policy. And if the leadership team should fail at any point to sustain progress toward that goal, the director added, then they are overpaid and should be replaced.

Top functional managers in strategically critical areas should be paid at the 75th percentile as well, the director said. Creating an information system that provides a competitive market advantage is an essential part of the growth strategy, he noted. Therefore, the MIS vice president should not be someone who is average for a $50-million company, but should bring the skills needed to attain much more ambitious strategic goals.

While this reasoning suited this particular business, other companies with different strategic intentions and compensation philosophies might well reason differently.

Expanding the Market-Value Criteria. Though market value criteria are fundamental to evaluating a job, many businesses use them only as a starting point.

Increasingly, compensation consultants and others are weighing so-called "qualitative criteria" in evaluating jobs. This approach considers the leadership, communication and integrative abilities demanded by a job. It incorporates nuances relating not only to the scope of the job but to the capabilities required to do it well. Incorporating these criteria into compensation planning can afford businesses a powerful tool to reinforce qualities and efforts that are crucial to achieving strategic goals. (Please see Table 6.)

These additional considerations hold that some jobs are more valuable than others because they require more of the individual. How much does the person in the job influence the strategy of the unit? How much does the employee interact with other parts of the business, and at what level? Is the job entirely internal, or does he or she represent the business to the outside world? At what level are the outsiders he or she deals with? Are they presidents of companies, staff people or warehouse workers? The answers to all of these questions can be qualitative factors in setting pay.

Some businesses tap compensation consultants to assess these nuances because they want to look beyond "market value" criteria. Other businesses use these criteria to assess jobs for which market data is difficult to determine. Most of all, these "qualitative" criteria are valuable in career planning discussions. The business owner can explain to a developing manager that more pay will be awarded as the person's performance grows in certain qualitative ways. Such discussions can be

TABLE 6

QUALITATIVE CRITERIA FOR VALUING JOBS

- Leadership characteristics: The degree of responsibility to create, communicate and execute the corporate strategy and vision.

- Command of subject matter required.

- Integrative requirements: The need to integrate different areas of the company, to integrate the business with the outside world, or to integrate information from multiple sources.

- Scope of internal and external contacts: The number of people the manager works with, the level of those contacts inside and outside the company, and the purpose of the contacts.

invaluable to an employee trying to understand the company's priorities and to plan his or her career path within that context.

Establishing Incentive Plans

While they may pay salespeople on commission or production workers by piece work, most small and medium-sized family businesses have no formal, distinct incentive system for their managers and executives.

But as businesses grow, owners sometimes consider giving bonuses as a way of tying pay to the business's performance, or to an individual's particular contribution to business performance. **"We really want to develop a culture around here wherein everybody does well when the company does well,"** one business owner reasoned when developing an incentive plan. "And when the company doesn't do well, we all sacrifice. We're not hiring bureaucrats here. We want people willing to share risk."

Tying compensation too closely to performance brings risks, however. Employees in certain roles have little individual ability to influence profits. To tie their pay too closely to performance could create undeserved windfalls or lead to the loss of important people, such as a top-performing director of information systems. For instance, a CEO's decision to do some aggressive strategic spending one year for future payoff shouldn't cause personal setbacks for employees who may have contributed to operating-profit gains but played no role in the CEO's decisions.

Nevertheless, the incentive principle can be helpful in compensation planning. The more weight given to bonuses, the closer the relationship between compensation and business performance.

Structuring Incentives. Neither the perfect incentive plan nor one "right way to do it" exists. An objective plan encourages employees to develop a certain outlook, attitude or set of behaviors that will help the company achieve strategic goals. With experience, the business owner can tie incentives to some very specific and crucial objectives.

An incentive plan based on business performance, of course, requires defining the levels of performance — outstanding, good, below average, etc. To define these terms, a business should look to business performance data in its industry — or, if not available, for companies in general. (Industry studies or *Inc.* or *Fortune* magazines are good sources.)

By definition, "outstanding" performance should be special in the industry and infrequent for the company. For example, if average after-tax return on equity in the industry (or in the business at large) is 13 percent, then "outstanding" might be an ROE of greater than, say, 20 percent, assuming the company would only be expected to achieve that ROE infrequently — perhaps one out of every three years. Other criteria also can be used, such as sales growth or project-dollar growth.

If the maximum target is high by industry standards but is reached regularly, the target should be set higher. As a rule, "outstanding" performance should be something that occurs only rarely; "good" performance should occur somewhat more often; and "average" should define the minimum expected performance in most years.

Incentives are usually given in cash, unless the business already has begun distributing stock to employees or has a stock-option or phantom-stock arrangement in place, as discussed later in this booklet. Table 7 shows the share of compensation at different levels of management that is typically received in incentives.

Many family businesses put a cap on incentives to guard against windfall bonuses for reasons, such as swings in commodity prices or currency-translation rates, **that are beyond any manager's control.** The cap can always be removed at the discretion of the business owner or board to reward truly superlative performance.

Some businesses also reserve cash to pay discretionary bonuses

TABLE 7

SHARE OF COMPENSATION
TYPICALLY RECEIVED IN INCENTIVES

Business Performance	Outstanding	Good	Below Average
Top managers	50% - 75%	20% - 50%	0% - 20%
Middle to upper-middle managers	20% - 50%	10% - 30%	0% - 10%
Lower-middle to middle managers	20% - 30%	10% - 20%	0% - 10%

depending upon individual employees' progress toward established personal goals, such as developing a successor capable of doing your job, installing a new computer system, completing a building project within budget or developing an orientation program for new employees.

Short-Term vs. Long-Term Incentives. When a family business first adds an incentive plan, it is almost always based on short-term goals, such as improving annual profit, revenue or cash flow. Top executives' short-term incentives may be based on such indicators as return on equity. This encourages managers to look beyond annual profit to maximizing the use of assets.

A next step is to base part of managers' bonus on long-term goals, such as increases in shareholder value or book value over three-to-five years. A common starting point is that about one-half to two-thirds of a manager's incentive package is based on short-term criteria, while one-third to one-half is based on long-term criteria.

Individual vs. Team Performance. Many companies try to strike a balance between rewarding an employee for individual achievement or for the results achieved by the company as a team. If bonuses are based entirely on team results, top-performing individuals may grow discouraged or quit. On the other hand, tying bonuses too tightly to individual results can create a damaging level of internal competition. Some

TABLE 8

SOME BONUS INCENTIVE EXAMPLES

■ Company A believes the current year's profit levels are about normal. Any profit next year that exceeds this year's level will be shared with management. Twenty percent of the profit increase will be evenly divided among the top five managers. Ten percent of the profit gain will be evenly divided among the next 12 managers.

■ **Company B** has decided that its minimum pre-tax return on capital should be 15 percent, assuring shareholders of a reasonable return on their investment. One-third of the profits beyond that minimum return-on-capital threshold are placed in a pool to be distributed among executives. Half of these pooled profits are shared proportionate to executives' salaries — thereby rewarding team accomplishment. The other half is distributed at the discretion of the CEO, based upon each individual's achievements during the year.

■ **Company C** seeks to reward sales growth and customer satisfaction. Each executive gets a bonus based on a percentage of salary equal to the percentage increase in the company's total revenues that year. Each also receives $5,000 in additional bonus payments for each 10 percent reduction in customer returns or allowances.

■ **Company D** bases its formula on total dollar profit improvement over three years and pays out one-third of the earned bonus each year, always retaining two-thirds for the future.

businesses may fine-tune their compensation systems several times trying to balance individual and team effort.

Given all the potential variables, bonus incentive plans can differ widely from company to company. Some examples of companies' bonus incentive formulas are contained in Table 8.

The Importance of "Shareholder Value." Shareholder value is a concept that surfaces more often these days in discussing incentive plans.

Shareholders in public companies are pressing management and directors to tie executive pay more closely to shareholder value.

Research supports this idea. A 1992 study by Kevin J. Murphy, a compensation expert at Harvard University, suggests that companies that reward executives for stock-price increases with stock-based pay consistently perform better than those that do not. According to an academic concept called "agency theory," the greater the distance between the interests of shareholders and executives, the more poorly the business performs. When managers' interests are too far from those of the shareholders, the theory holds, they spend more time and money maintaining their personal security and control over shareholders. Shareholders also use up more corporate resources just to monitor managers' performance. In contrast, the more stock top managers own, the more they relate to owners' interests, and the better the company typically performs.

This research holds several lessons for family businesses:

■ A business owned and led by a few family members should typically perform better than as if its ownership were dispersed to the public.

■ When a family business has several family shareholders not employed in the business, tying executive compensation to the value of the company, or shareholder value, may be a good way to reassure shareholders that management is attending to their interests.

■ Business owners should consider ways to tie the compensation of key non-family executives more closely to changes in shareholder value.

■ Family businesses need to develop ways to measure changes in the value of the business.

Perquisites. A compensation plan also should include strategic goals for passing out perks such as company cars, country-club memberships, credit cards and the like. Will the company be in the middle of the market or above or below that range in handing out perks? Why? What does your philosophy on perks say about your company in relationship to the marketplace?

Some family businesses tend to be more generous with perks than other companies, sometimes to compensate employees for paying them at below-market rates. Perks may be seen as a paternalistic device for "taking care of our people" or an entitlement of family ownership. But management of perks should be consistent with the company's strategy and compensation plan. Companies that are trying to be low-cost producers, for instance, should be frugal in this area, too.

Communicating Your Compensation Plan

A compensation plan should be communicated to shareholders, employees and perhaps to other constituents in a way that makes the basis for pay decisions clear and ties it to broader corporate goals.

This communication can take place in individual sessions with employees, executive team meetings, staff meetings or family meetings. In larger companies, the compensation philosophy is often conveyed in written form as well.

The message may express relationships or tradeoffs among the business's various constituencies — shareholders, employees, customers, suppliers and perhaps the community. Above all, it should help everyone involved to understand how the company's pay philosophy helps it remain competitive.

Clear communication on pay is increasingly important amid growing public awareness of potential executive-pay abuses. New SEC guidelines requiring more complete executive-pay disclosure for publicly traded companies will heighten public awareness still more. (Please see Exhibit 5.) These developments may result in increased curiosity about executive pay, even within family businesses.

In trying to establish a compensation plan that is both fair and effective, many businesses have found it helpful to abide by one of the most enduring tests of the ethics of business activity: **Would this compensation system survive "the light of day?" If this compensation plan were exposed to all, would most see it as just, purposeful and having integrity?**

If so, the business owner can rest easy.

Putting Your Compensation Plan to Work

Let's take a look at how a typical family-business pay decision might be handled once compensation planning is complete.

An $8-million commercial printing establishment in the Northwest recently hired the founder's 28-year-old daughter, Carol, as its new controller. Previously, the company had a director of accounting who handled recordkeeping, while the founder-CEO handled financial decisions.

Carol has finished school with a bachelor's degree in accounting. She passed the CPA test and worked five years for a regional public accounting firm. Her brother joined the company 10 years ago after graduating from college and serves as vice president, production. A younger sister is still in school, getting an MBA after working on the West Coast for two years.

26

EXHIBIT 5 ▇▇▇▇▇▇▇▇▇▇▇▇▇▇▇▇▇▇▇▇▇▇▇▇▇▇▇▇▇

SEC Regulations on Disclosing Executive Pay

Securities and Exchange Commission rules effective in 1993 require public companies to disclose the following:

■ The amount and forms of compensation of the CEO and four highest-paid executives whose compensation is over $100,000;

■ How compensation decisions were made;

■ How compensation relates to corporate performance.

The five senior officers' compensation packages (including stock options) must be valued and related to corporate performance, and the boards' compensation committees must give a detailed, signed explanation of why they paid those top executives as they did.

What Should the Family Pay Carol? First, it's important to clarify: **The family doesn't pay Carol — the business does!** While a family member, the founder-father, will as CEO make the final decision, it's important to maintain clarity that Carol's pay is a business decision.

Here are the steps that should follow:

1. Determine average or median market value for the job title in similar businesses.

Range: $35,000 — $82,000
Quartile I: $38,000
Median: $49,000
Quartile IV: $65,000

2. Consider the company's compensation policy related to market value — Does the company pay at the 75th percentile? Above average? Median? Below average?

The company chooses to pay at the median rate of $49,000, but wants to reward profit improvements aggressively through bonuses.

3. Adjust the pay level for critical qualitative considerations.

The company chose to hire a controller to catch up to industry standards in computers and internal financial reporting. Therefore, paying at the median rate for the industry, $49,000, is still appropriate.

4. Consider whether an annual bonus plan is appropriate.

The company wants to reward managers as a team, so 10 percent of all year-to-year profit increases are shared among team members. This year's budget shows an expected $150,000 increase in profit, so $15,000 would be shared among the five key people. That's $3,000 each — or almost 6 percent of annual pay for Carol.

5. Decide whether some incentive based on individual goals is appropriate.

The company feels an equivalent annual bonus ($3,000) is appropriate for people who meet individual performance goals. Those goals are set by each manager, who establishes three individual performance goals annually. Because Carol is new, this program will begin for her the following year. In her first full year of employment, the company will "guarantee" her the annual bonus, in keeping with the company's standing policy.

6. Consider a long-term bonus plan.

The company doesn't feel the need for one now.

7. Conclusion.

Carol's starting pay will be at the $49,000 median for the industry. She is eligible for about $6,000 in annual bonus payments, composed of $3,000 if the management team delivers on its profit budget (or exceeds it) and an additional $3,000 that is guaranteed in her first full year under the individual performance bonus policy. Though no formal long-term incentive plan is offered, she already has, as a family member, a long-term incentive to increase shareholder value.

If the company were interested in encouraging a greater long-term orientation or commitment among its managers, it might develop a bonus based on multi-year profit growth, with a deferred payout.

III. *Aligning Family Expectations and Compensation Philosophy*

At a very early age, children begin to learn attitudes about money, wealth and pay that stay with them for a lifetime.

Some families begin early to shape children's expectations, to prepare them for rational and systematic compensation in the business later in life. At various stages of the child's development, they may answer such questions as:

■ How is compensation determined in our business?

■ How does it compare to what people are paid elsewhere?

■ How can my parents afford to live as they do?

■ Will I be able to live as well as my parents do?

■ How much does the business have to grow to support all members of the next generation who may want to work there?

As discussed below, many family businesses find that communicating early and clearly about compensation, even at risk of seeming to convey "bad news," is better than allowing family members to speculate or form their own opinions in private, or worse, to build false expectations. Here are some techniques:

Living Modestly. Parents who live a little beneath their means and stress saving typically rear children who are more responsible and realistic about money. This can be particularly important for a business-owning family with several children, when the benefits of business ownership may be shared more broadly in the future among several siblings' families.

If parents show a capacity for sacrifice, telling children they must save for a new television or vacation, children will accept such limits as a part of life. They will grow up able to make tradeoffs between saving and spending. A modest lifestyle can help children avoid an uncomfortable transition in the future, when the pay for the work they do may fall short of their parents' income.

Parents also should avoid conspicuous or excessive use of perks, not only to adhere to various IRS regulations, but to avoid raising children's expectations. We recommend against passing company credit cards for telephone calls or gasoline freely around the family. If they are, spending limits should be set.

Sending Clear Messages from the Beginning. Compensation can be a headache if children are brought up with distorted ideas about the meaning of their paychecks. As discussed in Section V of this booklet, using the family business as a conduit for a tax-deductible allowance to high school or college students can lead them to expect the same support as adults. It also can teach children questionable attitudes about paying taxes.

Many parents also have learned that it pays to guard against well-meaning offhand remarks, such as "Someday this business will all be yours," or "A family business is a money tree." While such comments may arise from an enthusiastic and understandable desire to interest the children in the business, they can backfire later in life. Children who learn to view leadership of the family business as a birthright or a source of unending cash have a high likelihood later of creating problems for the business — and for themselves.

Setting Entry-Level Pay. When a family member enters the business, there is no substitute for paying what the job is worth. This is also a good time to share some elements of the family-business compensation philosophy. The business owner might discuss how the company pays compared with the market and encourage questions about compensation. If a younger family member says, "I have a friend who works in construction who is making $12 an hour," the business owner might respond, "Well, that's what construction pays. For a warehouse job in our industry, the going rate is $7." If a family member with a particularly strong education or outside experience enters the business, some special compensation issues arise. Ideally, the family member can be hired into an existing position with a pay history worthy of his or her education or experience.

But often, family businesses don't have such jobs. One solution is to "subsidize" the family member's pay to reflect fairly his or her qualifications. One family business paid an entering family member with an MBA at the median rate for all the MBA graduates of his university. That was a way of reflecting the "fair market value" of that graduate's potential. If the family member has experience on top of the degree, higher pay may be warranted. Other businesses offer incentive pay for school performance. If the family member graduates in the top quarter of the class, he or she is paid as much as other graduates at that level.

The family member should be told how much of his or her pay is for the job, and how much of the pay is for a "training program" or based on "future potential." This enables the business to compete for individuals against other companies willing to pay them for their potential, but avoids sending mixed messages about the way jobs in the business are valued. The family member should also be told when the "training period" will end and prepared for the time when he or she will enter a job paid strictly at the market rate.

Families who believe strongly in the value of outside experience sometimes subsidize the pay of a family member while they work somewhere else. This pays the family member for his or her potential while permitting a period of "training" in a job beneath that potential. Again, the market value of the job performed should be made clear to the family member, as well as the reasons for the subsidy.

Talking about Income Sources. Another helpful step is to share income information with family members when they are young adults. How much of the money that supports the family lifestyle comes from investment income? How much from inheritance? How much from savings? How much comes from our current income from jobs in the family business? How much from dividends? Explaining these distinctions can help family members appreciate what it takes to sustain a certain standard of living, and that income sources other than the family-business paycheck can play a major role.

It also can help prepare members of the next generation for their own financial future. Many children grow up expecting to live at least as well, or better, than their parents. If the family lifestyle is supported by inherited wealth, real-estate investments or other sources, children should be prepared for the possibility of a decline in their standard of living — unless they, too, have or develop additional sources of income. Such talks may encourage them early to take a realistic view of their prospects in the family business.

Helping Family Members Plan Careers. Talking about compensation is a natural way to help family members plan careers within the business. As family members move up through the ranks, explaining the goals of the compensation system can help them set personal objectives. What qualities and abilities are most highly rewarded in our business? What skills will best equip you to aspire to the highest-ranking jobs, or the most attractive opportunities? A manager who develops the ability to deal with presidents of other companies has brighter career prospects than the mailroom supervisor who is only comfortable talking with staffers at the post office, for instance.

As discussed in Section IV of this booklet, a compensation consultant can help by conducting an orientation program. **One family business has children attend a compensation orientation session while they are in college.** The session offers an outline of the compensation philosophy of the business and a description of how the value of a job is determined. Career counseling can be offered at this stage as well. This not only helps offspring plan their own future, but gives them a chance to feel like trusted part-owners of the enterprise.

Parting the Curtain on Future Pay. As the next generation of family-business owners enters their late 20s and early 30s, many parents begin to discuss the philosophy and structure of future family ownership and pay. Will all siblings or cousins be paid based on the market value of their job, or equally as members of a partnership? Or will one be assigned chief-executive responsibility and paid more? Is the family member a potential candidate for that job? How will entrepreneurial contributions be rewarded? This information can help the young family member plan a career path that will meet not only his or her personal goals, but pay aspirations as well.

As family members marry, their spouses should be fully informed about family and business approaches to compensation. If family members are paid differently, spouses may become suspicious or resentful. Explaining the pay system to them privately, through family meetings or by providing written minutes of board meetings, can help reduce the potential for conflict.

Avoiding the Christmas Bonus. With the best of intentions, many entrepreneurs form a habit of offering employees a Christmas bonus. This can take on symbolic meaning through the years and become a powerful tool for shaping expectations — often in ways the business owner comes to regret.

Early in the life of the business, the owner may use a gift of a holiday turkey or cash to express gratitude to employees for "hanging in there" through tough times. In good years, he or she may feel like sharing the wealth, again as an expression of gratitude. This is particularly common among entrepreneurs who may not be comfortable giving other kinds of positive feedback.

Once the habit is formed, it is hard to stop without creating disappointment or misunderstandings. As the company grows, the Christmas bonus may expand to burdensome proportions if it has nothing to do with company or individual performance. Employees come to expect it. They grow resentful if it doesn't come, or if it is smaller than expected.

Such precedents often linger even after a company adopts a rational compensation policy. The Christmas check may be transformed into a profit-sharing contribution or a cash bonus system, but it still remains "the Christmas check" at its core. The same problem can develop with pension plans that are not tied to a formula based on company profits. These "entitlements" can haunt future generations who may want to discard them in favor of a more objective, merit-based system, but who may be forced by the older generation or employee pressure to retain them.

In our opinion, the best solution is never to start giving Christmas bonuses.

IV. *Special Issues*

Compensation planning touches so many aspects of the family business that it often raises a variety of other issues. Here is a summary of a few of them.

Compensation as a Catalyst for Other Crucial Planning

One reason compensation planning can be difficult is that it often unearths major unresolved issues.

Developing a compensation philosophy that ties pay to the goals and mission of the business requires the business owner to articulate those goals. That demands a foundation of sound strategic planning, an effort that may have to be completed before compensation plans can be laid.

Compensation planning also can raise questions about whether the CEO's pay and savings are sufficient to assure a financially secure, independent retirement. This can lead to a personal financial planning effort for the CEO and spouse which in turn often raises estate-planning questions.

Compensation planning also can raise questions about family members' role in the business and their collective mission as shareholders. As compensation is shifted to a more rational foundation, many families find it necessary to re-unite as shareholders behind a newly articulated statement of mission or values. The result is what is often called a family mission statement or creed, or simply a family plan, as discussed in No. 2 of The Family Business Leadership Series, *Family Meetings: How to Build a Stronger Family and a Stronger Business*.

These four plans — the personal financial plan, the estate plan, the strategic plan and the family plan — form the cornerstones of sound family-business leadership and continuity through generations. Compensation planning frequently stimulates these planning efforts, and in fact can seldom be completed without them.

Retiring Family Executives

Ideally, a retiring CEO has planned and accumulated enough resources to sustain an independent retirement. As he or she hands over responsibility and authority to the next generation, pay can be scaled down accordingly. In this ideal model, the business owner is paid what he or she is worth right up to the last minute. He or she should not take more than needed, because anything not consumed will be heavily taxed if left in the estate at death.

But that's usually not the way it happens. Most retirees have not developed enough financial independence to sever their financial ties with the business. Many make the mistake of simply staying on the payroll. This not only compromises the compensation system, but it can raise awkward questions about annual reviews and pay increases in a company trying to take a systematic approach to compensation.

A better solution may be to develop a consulting agreement for the departing CEO. A retiree may feel proud of such an arrangement. It allows him or her to sustain dignity and a sense of importance while achieving independence and control over personal time. It also allows the next generation to set a time limit on the cash outlay, while giving the retiring CEO adequate time to achieve financial security. A consulting contract might contain a provision that would continue benefits and partial payment under the contract to a surviving spouse, in case the retired CEO dies.

Ideally, the consulting arrangement should be as much like an arm's-length agreement as possible, priced at the market and evaluated by the executive committee or the board. In one case, a retiring CEO's long-term consulting agreement, entitling him to annual revenue equal to his salary at retirement, was set for review by the board every five years. The agreement, the board's compensation committee noted in its minutes, "reflects the value of (the retiring CEO's) role to the company." This honored the CEO while preserving people's respect for the compensation system.

Unfortunately, many retiring CEOs object to the idea of a consulting arrangement. Many find almost intolerable the idea that a successor is making more money than they are. This can force a family business into the costly situation of keeping a retired CEO on a salary that is continually rising to stay ahead of a successor's. In the worst cases, the CEO also continues to work part-time, interfering with successors' autonomy, and holds onto all the stock in the business as well. Such an arrangement can jeopardize the financial and strategic health of the business.

Again, shaping expectations can be helpful in avoiding such problems. Many family businesses beginning a systematic effort to plan for succession find that personal financial planning for the retiring CEO is an essential component. At that point, an active outside board or other trusted outside advisor can be of enormous help in identifying various financial options for retirement.

An active board can help smooth the retirement process. The departing CEO might be given a board fee or honorarium for acting as chairman emeritus. Though the retiree would not vote or even necessarily attend meetings, the board fee provides a way of channelling funds to him or her. The drawback is that this method risks people's respect for director compensation.

Compensating Nonfamily Executives

Rewarding and retaining key nonfamily executives can be a continuing challenge for family businesses.

Using stock to compensate key managers is a tempting idea. It is an obvious way to tie compensation to the long-term value of the business — an idea many family businesses find appealing because of their long-term orientation. Also, handing out stock can seem a cheap way to reward key people. The idea is increasingly topical as more public companies use stock and derivative products in executive-pay packages.

But stock ownership should never be discussed casually with nonfamily employees. Offhand remarks can come back to haunt you. A business owner trying hard to lure a top recruit may drop a reference to the possibility that he or she "might own stock someday." Most business owners don't really want to grant stock ownership when "someday" comes. But many find that their casual hint has been transformed in the mind of the recruit into a promise, raising expectations — and major problems. Family businesses that are considering offering stock to nonfamily employees should formulate a policy before even raising the issue.

Because they usually want to restrict ownership to family members, most family businesses ultimately decide not to grant stock to nonfamily members. Moreover, by the use of so-called "phantom stock," incentives can be offered without conferring rights of ownership.

Phantom or Shadow Stock. Other business owners try to get nonfamily executives to "think like owners" without actually owning stock by using equity substitutes such as "phantom" or "shadow" stock. The value of phantom stock is tied to changes in the value of the business. The formula might be based on changes in book value, on a price-earnings (P/E) ratio as compared with the industry, or on some other measure of shareholder value.

For many family businesses, book value is the simplest and easiest-to-explain indicator. While book value is often understated, it still works fine as a "weather vane" for changes in the company's value without reflecting the wild and often irrelevant swings of the financial markets. Larger family businesses may hire an independent valuation specialist to value the company based on all three indicators — book value, P/E ratio and estimated market value.

Phantom stock allows the nonfamily executive to participate in any rise in the value of the business without actually owning a stake. In the family business, this approach can lessen the "us-versus-them" attitude that can develop among employees who may feel cut off from ownership. It also can encourage employees to think about long-term goals.

Other Tools. Family businesses use a variety of other ways to reward nonfamily executives.

Some family firms give nonfamily key executives **unusually high pay, perks or incentives**, in an effort to make up for their inability to acquire stock or to rise to the CEO position in a family-run business. This technique can go awry, however, if it results in increased secrecy or perceived inequities. In its most negative variation, the business owner might also make a point of frequently reminding the nonfamily executive of his or her high pay, in an implied threat or implicit demand for loyalty.

Deferred compensation is a potentially more constructive technique. To encourage the nonfamily executive to remain with the company, some business owners put income into a deferred compensation plan that may take five, ten or more years to vest. Even after vesting, some businesses make the money available only after the manager quits or retires.

While deferred compensation, often called "golden handcuffs," can provide an incentive to stay with a business, it can backfire by driving executives to quit to get the cash. Some businesses make at least some of the money available earlier as a morale booster. Other firms always defer the compensation by three to five years. Asking for help from a compensation consultant or other professional advisor is usually wise when constructing complex compensation packages.

Participation in family investments is another option. Business-owning families may join in investment opportunities such as foreign stocks, warehouse or equipment leasing, or real estate. Nonfamily executives may be allowed to participate as well, usually in one of two ways. They may be allowed to invest at a discount, or they can participate in any investment gains for free. The problem with the first way is that it requires the nonfamily executive to risk personal funds based on the family's investment decisions. He or she may be reluctant to do so, and equally reluctant to tell the family why. The latter alternative gives the nonfamily manager the upside potential of the family investment, without exposing him or her to the downside risk.

Other family businesses allow nonfamily executives to own franchises or shares in related business units, suppliers or retail outlets for the company. This affords them an opportunity to participate in the benefits of ownership without diluting the family's equity stake in the parent.

Table 9 summarizes the pros and cons of a variety of ways of rewarding nonfamily executives.

Compensating Family and Nonfamily Directors

The same principles that guide compensation should rule directors' fees. Though abuses are common — with directors' fees being used to save on taxes or channel compensation to needy family members, for instance — directors' compensation should reflect "market values." The fee paid family directors should convey the significance of their role. If the board is inactive and a rubber stamp for the CEO, then membership should pay little or nothing. Otherwise, over time, family members will lose respect for the business and all its pay policies.

Role confusion is common, again because family directors sometimes play multiple roles — as owners, employees and board members. Briefly, family members who manage the company and also serve on the board should receive no board fees. Customary business practice dictates that board service is part of top managers' jobs. Their interaction with other directors is valuable partly because of their knowledge and understanding as managers of the business. If family members who do not work in the business are also on the board, they usually should be paid the same as outside directors.

Other questions may arise. A family member who is a shipping room clerk, but is also a director for family reasons, obviously isn't present on the board because he or she is a top manager. If the clerk is seen as representing family interests on the board, rather than simply attending as an inside director, he or she might be compensated for serving. (To maintain the integrity of the pay system and the board, the clerk should probably take unpaid time off for attending board meetings.) Similarly, a family member elected or chosen by other family members to represent family interests on the board may deserve to be compensated as an outside director.

TABLE 9

INCENTIVES FOR KEY NON-FAMILY EXECUTIVES

Concept	Advantages	Disadvantages
Discretionary Bonus	■ Encourages clear goal-setting and comprehensive review.	■ Rarely done well; usually uncomfortable for both parties.
Discretionary Perquisites	■ Strengthens personal-family ties.	■ Others may be offended; can create paternalism.
Annual Profit Bonus	■ Related to ability to pay and to company performance	■ Not long-term oriented; profits can be affected by uncontrollable events.
Long-Range or Multi-Year Profit Bonus	■ Ties employee to company longer; encourages more long-term view.	■ Profits don't necessarily measure most important criteria (i.e., return on equity, market share, etc.)
Phantom Stock	■ Long-term orientation and related to shareholder benefit.	■ Difficult to value for private company.
Real Common Stock	■ Long-term orientation and related to shareholder benefit. Confers greater emotional meaning or status.	■ Complicated legal administration and difficult to value.
Non-Company Investment Opportunities	■ Strengthens personal-family ties. Doesn't affect company's stock ownership.	■ Not readily available. Any failure brings major disappointment.

SOME COMMON REASONS FOR HIRING A COMPENSATION CONSULTANT

- You want to set up an organization-wide incentive program.

- You want to overhaul compensation in favor of a rational system.

- Family shareholders not employed in the business start asking questions about pay.

- You find yourself giving all employees almost the same raises every year.

- You begin losing key nonfamily executives.

- Your outside board says you need one.

Using a Compensation Consultant

Many family businesses, particularly smaller firms, tap an accountant or outside directors for objective advice and counsel. Other, larger firms may use a compensation consultant. Some common reasons are listed in Table 10.

If you turn to a compensation consultant, trying to negotiate prices is always advisable. As part of your total package, here are some additional services you might request:

- a procedure manual;

- an evaluation of perks;

- a presentation to directors, executives or shareholders on the findings and recommendations;

- training or orientation sessions for employees or family members;

- a review of special issues such as director or sales-force compensation;

- in larger companies, an annual review for one or more years to evaluate and fine-tune the system — for no extra charge. (Smaller firms probably won't need a consultant's advice more often than every two to three years.)

IV. *Building Trust*

A key to an effective compensation system is building trust among family members, employees and others. Here are some issues that often arise as business owners try to build trust in the compensation planning process.

Making Pay an Open Book Among Family Members

Many family business owners are most comfortable keeping pay secret. Unfortunately, that doesn't prevent family members from forming strong opinions, suspicions and beliefs about pay anyway. This **uninformed speculation is almost always more extreme and damaging than the truth.**

Compensation policy should be an open book among family members. Questions about pay inevitably arise among siblings or cousins in or out of the business, and spouses need to be informed as well. Unless compensation policy is explained, through family meetings or in written minutes of board meetings, spouses may grow angry and resentful over pay or lifestyle differences — a problem that can reverberate through management.

As the family begins moving in this direction, disclosure of any information about individuals' pay should be discreet and consistent with company policy. Any steps toward casting light on subjects that in the past have been secret should be gradual and respectful of individuals' privacy rights.

Ideally, the new generation might get involved in planning a compensation system. One way to do that is to let them become a task force that proposes a compensation plan either to the CEO or to the CEO and the board, or recommends changes to an existing plan.

The Role of an Outside Board

If a family business has an active outside board of directors or panel of advisors, a good first step is to disclose compensation practices to them. In the confidential setting of the boardroom, a business owner can use directors as a sounding board. Directors can review and react to the owner's plans, or help evaluate advice from an accountant or compensation consultant. Their reaction often helps the CEO gain confidence about the basis for pay decisions and become more adept at communicating it.

In subjecting a compensation philosophy to review by a trusted board, the business owner also gains credibility with other family members. Once this practice is established, the CEO, executive committee or top-management team should try to articulate the company's philosophy of compensation and go over it with the board once a year.

In one fast-growing family enterprise, a dispute over compensation of family members in the business actually helped spark formation of an active outside board. Dismayed by criticism from family members not active in the business, managers brought all the family shareholders together to select a panel of trusted outside directors who might help assess the executive pay package, make changes and communicate a compensation plan to inactive family members. The management team also hired a compensation consultant to provide recommendations and reliable data to the board.

The result: A restoration of trust and confidence among family members. The directors helped educate shareholders about pay; oversaw plans to buy back some holders' shares; articulated a compensation philosophy much like that of a professionally managed public company; and defused some contentious issues, such as the windfall bonuses paid in some extraordinarily good years in the past, by setting a bonus "cap" that could be removed at directors' discretion. Board minutes were made available to shareholders, and directors reviewed compensation and compensation philosophy annually at a family shareholder meeting.

In larger businesses, the board often forms a compensation committee of outside directors. This group reviews annual salary, bonus and other benefits for the CEO and other officers or senior managers and ratifies the CEO's compensation decisions. Members also can be asked to review perks, benefits and pension plans, and to help tie compensation to the company's culture, goals and mission.

Using Compensation as a Foundation for Business Education

Many employees assume that if a business is profitable, it has plenty of surplus cash for pay raises. Some family businesses use that perception as a starting point to help employees learn more about the business. They may teach employees — and shareholders, too, when appropriate — to understand finance and strategy issues through seminars, written materials, informal talks or other means. These efforts can help derail stereotypes about "obscene profits" or "fat bonuses" by exploring such questions as:

- What is return on investment, and why does a business need to maintain a higher rate of return than less risky investments such as Treasury bills?

- If the performance of the business helps guide pay policy, then how do we know how well the business is performing? Do we look at profits? Return on investment? Sales growth?

- What happens to profit? Is it deposited in the bank, or reinvested in the business? If so, for what?

- What kinds of business cycles affect our industry? Why isn't it safe to assume that if profits are abundant one year, the same factors will lead to high profits the next?

- How do profits at our company compare to others in our industry and to companies in other industries?

These discussions lay the groundwork for communicating a philosophy of compensation. What are the company's priorities in allocating resources among employees, customers, stockholders and suppliers? Is our first priority to create a supportive environment for employees by plowing profits into pay and benefits? To increase shareholder value by reinvesting in business assets? To spend money on process improvements that will lower costs to customers? Understanding these tradeoffs can be a major step toward teamwork among family members and other employees.

Separating Pay and Performance Reviews

A common practice is to review an employee's pay and performance at the same meeting. Some business owners reason that this approach "gets it all over with," avoiding the need to sit down twice for confidential discussions with an employee over issues that can make both people uncomfortable.

A significant disadvantage, though, is that performance issues and coaching opportunities are lost amid both participants' preoccupation with pay. "How am I going to tell this person about her pay raise?" the boss may be wondering, while the employee worries, "What does all this mean to my paycheck?"

A better method may be to separate the discussions into two sessions six months apart, with a pay review in, say, December, and a performance review in May or June. When separated from the question of pay, the performance review is easier, particularly for family-business owners who may particularly dislike discussing compensation. The performance review becomes the coaching experience it needs to be.

The separate compensation session then becomes an opportunity to educate the employee on how his or her pay is determined and how it relates to the performance of the business. In this discussion, the business owner can explain aspects of compensation philosophy that will encourage the employee to develop skills and make career plans that mesh with the business's strategic goals.

Relating Performance to Pay

A technique that works well for some family businesses in teaching the concept of performance-based pay is to have siblings sit down together once or twice a year as a team and evaluate their performance to each other. This doesn't mean they evaluate each other. Instead, they assess their own performance in each other's presence, based on the goals they have set for themselves in cooperation with the CEO, a key manager or the board.

Each family member might tell his or her team members, for instance, "Here are my objectives for the year, and here is what I think would be an accomplishment sufficient to justify a bonus of 10 percent, based on my objectives." Then at the end of the year, the group would sit down together again to revisit those objectives as compared with each family member's actual accomplishments. The purpose is to begin a dialog and establish a pattern of openness and an adherence to performance-based pay criteria that will sustain the team members throughout their work together in the business. This open sharing of goals and progress provides motivation through peer group accountability.

An alternative would be for each sibling to delegate responsibility for their performance review to the rest of the team members. Note that the responsibility should be freely given. Siblings should not be subjected to involuntary peer review and criticism.

Sticking to the System

Just as football plays fail if one player wanders away, compensation plans lose credibility if exceptions are made. Any break in agreed-upon practice sends a message that the compensation philosophy does not apply equally to everyone and therefore cannot be trusted.

Staying the course can be difficult. One second-generation family business we know had brought several offspring into the business. All were married with children and working in lower- or middle-management jobs. All were paid modest salaries under a compensation plan that applied to all employees. Dividends from their shareholdings in the family business brought their total income to a level where they could enjoy a modestly comfortable lifestyle and save a little. All thought of themselves as living on "a limited budget," and none aspired to great wealth.

But as the family began planning for a successor to the business's 51-year-old CEO and founder, a question arose. One promising candidate, a brother working in another industry, had been successful and was making a salary in six figures. But inviting him into the business meant offering him a lower-ranking job so he could "earn his stripes," learn the family business culture and work his way up, in keeping with the company's policy of promoting from within. It also would mean a pay cut of more than 50 percent.

The question came to a standoff. The brother was willing to take the lower-level job the family offered, but only if it did not mean a pay cut. And the family was willing to try creative solutions to recruit a potential family successor, but not to compromise the integrity of the compensation system. The result: The brother stayed at his high-paying job, and the family turned in their search to nonfamily candidates. All involved remained on friendly terms, largely because the family was sticking to an established, agreed-upon compensation policy.

In this case, where the brother's qualifications for leadership were still untested, any other answer would have meant destroying the integrity of the compensation system.

Anticipating Issues That May Arise

Most enduring family businesses hit compensation trouble spots. Awareness of these potholes can help the business owner develop policies in advance to deal with them. A sampling of "sticking points" is contained in Table 11.

Another way of anticipating compensation issues is to understand the changes family businesses go through as they pass from the first to second and subsequent generations of family ownership. As discussed in No. 2 of The Family Business Leadership Series, *Family Meetings*, each

47

TABLE 11

COMMON COMPENSATION TROUBLE SPOTS

- The entry of younger children into the business. If the discrepancies among children's paychecks are too great, parents may have to explain why.

- The advent of the first generation of family stockholders who are *not* working in the business. These family members may question or resent others' pay.

- The desire to recruit a highly qualified or experienced family member from outside the business. Pay decisions on this recruit may seem to insiders to "break the mold," raising questions or resentments.

- A decision to try to attract nonfamily managers. This raises questions about compensation, perks, incentives and stock ownership.

- The retirement of a business owner who continues to draw a paycheck. Successors' frustration over their inability to control payroll costs can lead them to try to rope the ex-CEO into compensation planning.

- An entrepreneur's frustration that employees expect routine annual pay raises regardless of the business's profits. This often sparks a plan to tie pay more closely to company performance.

- A change in the nature of the business. Examples: a shift to a team sales approach from one that emphasizes individual superstars, or the emergence of low-paid customer-service people, rather than salespeople, as critical to the company's growth.

of the three stages in family-business evolution — the founding or entrepreneurial stage, the sibling ownership stage, and the "cousin" or "family dynasty" stage — raises new issues of family participation, team-building and shareholder unity. Similarly, each of these new stages tends to create certain predictable questions about pay.

Here is a summary of some of the pay issues most common to businesses in each stage.

The Entrepreneurial Stage. Compensation can seem simple when the business is run by the founder or by one offspring of the founder, and the next generation is only beginning to enter the business. At this stage, parents set the culture and the tone of any discussions about compensation. Attitudes toward saving on taxes, family gifting, phantom jobs and other pay practices are conveyed and absorbed uncritically by offspring. With one or two people in unquestioned control, few conflicts erupt.

One issue that may arise is whether parents have sufficient savings to ensure their security in retirement. If parents lack an adequate retirement cushion, that needs to be communicated to the next generation and resolved. Estate planning can raise the same issues.

If parents *are* financially secure independent of the business, they also need to let the next generation know that. The way the message is conveyed, however, can either enhance or distort children's understanding of compensation. If children are allowed to believe that the business owner's salary was the sole source of the wealth accumulated over the years, they may form unrealistic expectations about their own income potential in the business. On the other hand, the business owner can use the opportunity to inform children about the difference between compensation and dividends or other sources of wealth.

The Sibling or Second-Generation Stage. A large number of second-generation family businesses today are owned and managed by a team of siblings. Some embrace a "partnership vision" whereby two to four siblings co-own and co-lead the business with very few, if any, inactive family shareholders or nonfamily shareholders. Some prefer to choose a new leader from among several siblings.

Complaints about compensation often arise at this stage, but that does not necessarily mean that the underlying resentments or inequities did not exist before. It may mean only that the presence of older family members was such a powerful influence that younger members did not focus on, or feel free to express, their questions or concerns.

Several issues are common. Do the children view the family business as a money tree rather than a proving ground? How does the family deal with differences in lifestyle? Are children prepared for the fact that multiple siblings will lead the business in the future, and for the questions about compensation that raises? If a son enters the business as expected and is awarded an artificially high and ever-increasing rate of pay, what happens 15 years later when another son opts for a family-business career and begins wondering why he can't earn the same exalted salary? What perks are fair and how will they be allotted? How will information about compensation be communicated among family members?

Ideally, the parent generation has already shaped the pay expectations of second-generation leaders as they enter the business. In one family business, the principle that siblings would be paid differently based on the nature of their jobs and their backgrounds, among other things, was accepted. Yet all were aware that the policy posed risks to the team's relationships. When the three brothers in the business began speculating about pay behind each other's backs, they were offered a chance to meet to discuss their questions, with the help of the outside board's compensation committee. The brothers' right to privacy was respected; the meeting was presented as a voluntary team-building effort, and no one was pressured to participate. All three chose to take part, and the result was a candid, relaxed exchange.

One by one, the brothers discussed their pay, the reasons for it and any frustrations with it. The youngest was making more than the middle brother because he was paid at the median for his graduating class at his high-ranking MBA school. But his bonus potential in his current job is limited, he told his brothers.

The middle brother admitted some discomfort over his lower pay, but supported the principles behind it. His job offered more bonus potential, and he told his brothers of his plans to increase his base pay by expanding his job responsibilities.

The oldest brother said he was happy with the broad management, line and strategic responsibility afforded by his job. Though his bonus was up to 25 percent of his pay, he said he would like even greater incentive opportunities.

After each had spoken, all discussed with directors some key characteristics of jobs that justify higher pay levels. They also talked about threats to their team relationship. Though odds were against harmony, all the brothers said they were committed to making it work. "If we fail, I would feel I had failed," one brother said.

The discussion defused suspicions and heightened the brothers' commitment to teamwork. It also underscored to each man how important their relationship was to each of them and laid the groundwork for honest, open and mutually respectful communications in the future.

The Third-Generation or "Cousin" Stage. Toward the end of the sibling stage or at the third generation of family-business ownership, a new era begins. At this point, all shareholders usually are no longer employed in the business. The family business begins to resemble a public company. It becomes increasingly important for the managers of the business to be fair to all family members.

The advent of owners who lack day-to-day contact with the business can raise issues that transform the compensation system — or sometimes, wreak havoc with it. Family shareholders may begin to suspect that their siblings or cousins in the business are overpaid, at the expense of their dividends or shareholder value. They may begin speculating or trying to conduct their own independent pay assessment.

Family members not in leadership roles rarely appreciate the unique emotional burdens of leadership. They usually underestimate top managers' sense of stewardship for their interests. They also don't realize the degree to which top executives "live the job" mentally and socially, reflecting on business problems and attending business-related gatherings during their "time off." The person who understands these unspoken pressures best is the top executive's spouse. And he or she is likely to resent any indignation that may arise among siblings about executive pay. Therein lie the seeds of conflict that can eventually pull apart a family business — and a family.

These pressures often lead second- or third-generation family businesses to move toward a rational, open and professional compensation plan similar to those embraced by publicly held companies. At this stage, an external source of information and advice, such as a compensation consultant, an active outside board or both, is often necessary to win the trust of active and inactive shareholders alike.

Other questions arise at this stage about how to reward both owners and employees fairly. As growth in the family dilutes individuals' equity stakes, managers may need additional incentives, beyond their existing ownership of shares, to build shareholder value. This may lead to a long-term incentive plan tied to measures based upon increases in shareholder value.

Coping with Unequal Lifestyles

Maintaining family harmony can be difficult if siblings' or cousins' standards of living diverge. And that is inevitable in third-stage companies when the ages of offspring are very different.

Family shareholders not working in the business may resent a sister whose compensation as the family-business CEO enables her to live on Luxury Lane. A 21-year-old sibling just starting out in the business as a shipping clerk may only be able to afford a one-bedroom apartment, while his parents and 31-year-old brother, an executive vice president and heir apparent, are living in $500,000 houses. The resulting discord may harm both the business and the family.

This problem afflicts many family businesses. Some families buoy everyone up through dividends or gifts. This strategy maintains the integrity of the compensation system by avoiding mixed messages on the value of the family member's job. But it risks compromising the future financial strength of the business. Other families add a "family allowance" of, say, $20,000 a year to each family member's paycheck. In addition to draining cash from the business, this method tends to distort family pay in top management. A CEO who should by rights be making $200,000 may feel guilty taking more, for instance. So he or she may reduce base salary so that net pay, after the family allowance, is still only $200,000.

In another case, a family specifically distinguished "compensation from executive committee involvement" from "ownership return" from the business and a family trust. This family also made "equal wealth" rather than equal income the goal for family members. Given that the family collectively had far more wealth at stake as owners than as employees, members set a goal of each contributing to the family's combined wealth. In return, family members received a constant level of income to meet "accustomed lifestyles," in addition to their pay from performing a job in the business and any appropriate bonuses. Each member also received an equal fee for participating in the executive committee of the business. The result: a pay system that supported family members in a chosen lifestyle, primarily through "family income" and the fee for executive committee participation. Though this approach may have diminished the importance to family members of their job paychecks, it did not violate the integrity of the compensation system.

In summary, easing tensions over unequal lifestyles almost always involves tradeoffs. Is shareholder harmony and commitment valuable enough to risk a certain degree of the business's financial strength? Whatever the decision, the issue should be addressed head-on, preferably through a policy that has been developed in advance.

Family Meetings and Family Vacations

Family meetings or shareholder gatherings are often advisable at this stage to discuss family and business issues, as discussed in No. 2 of The Family Business Leadership Series, *Family Meetings*. These gatherings can raise questions about paying family members' travel and other expenses so they can attend. Larger businesses often view these reimbursements as the cost of maintaining "shareholder relations" and keeping shareholders informed. This levels the playing field among family members working in the business, who likely have business expense accounts to cover their costs, and those who are not active in the business.

Usually, all legitimate expenses should be covered, including babysitters or travel costs from great distances. This may mean paying different amounts to different family members. If questions arise, it can be helpful to remember that the cost and location of a family meeting is beyond the control of inactive shareholders. They should not be penalized for the distance they have to travel or other arrangements they may have to make as a result.

Ten Easy Ways to Destroy Trust in Your Compensation Plan

Let's take a close look at some very common and often unconscious mistakes that can prevent the business owner from reaching this important goal.

Pitfall One: Confusing Family and Business Roles. Members of business families play many roles in relation to each other. Individuals' family roles, their business ownership stakes, their involvement in community activities — all are frequently confused with the *job they do* when deciding what they should be paid.

One family-business owner, a vice president-sales in a subsidiary of a large business, asked an advisor, "I own 13 percent of the stock in our company. What should I be paid?" When told that he should be paid at a rate comparable to other sales VP's in similar companies, he looked puzzled.

Family members may ask, "I guess cousins are paid less than sons or daughters?" Similarly, owners may remark, "My son is getting $125,000 a year. I don't know what the market rate for his job would be, but it doesn't matter because he's an owner," or, "I know my daughter is paid more than others at her level, but she has been so helpful to us and needs the extra cash." These remarks confuse compensation with dividends to owners or gifts to needy family members.

This role confusion can destroy the integrity of family business compensation. And it wastes the potential of pay as a strategic tool.

Pitfall Two: Using Pay Primarily to Achieve Tax Savings. For some family businesses, saving on taxes is a primary goal. This is most often true when most employees are family members, the structure of the business is informal and profits are tight. In lieu of a compensation plan, the entrepreneur may sit down with an accountant and try to figure out ways to get some money out of the business. Many family businesses inflate salaries to family members as a way of increasing cash flow to shareholders in the most tax-advantaged way. (Payroll costs are deductible as a business expense. In contrast, dividends in a C corporation are taxed twice, and gifts or inheritances come from after-tax dollars and may require heavy gift or estate taxes as well.)

For instance, families may view the salary of high-school or college students employed in the business as a "tax-deductible allowance." Instead of giving children the money they need from their own after-tax income, these parents see it as cheaper to overcompensate them in the family business. Many businesses also use perks to transfer money from the business to family members in a tax-advantaged way. Country club dues, company cars, travel and car telephones are deductible as business expenses but are not taxed to the individual. Others pad the payroll with "phantom jobs" that provide income, health insurance or other benefits for needy family members. **When people who don't do their jobs show up on the payroll, others both inside and outside the firm lose respect for the company.**

Whatever the rewards, these techniques harm the integrity of the compensation system, as well as raising potential illegalities, and send a distorted message that can erupt into problems later. It's a happy circumstance when a family has enough resources to conduct financial affairs in a clean and straightforward way. **Many find that paying the associated taxes is less costly in the long run than cultivating distorted expectations about pay.**

Pitfall Three: Using Pay to Maintain Parental Control. Many parents use pay to achieve goals that have nothing to do with the job. They may use big paychecks to lure children into the family business or keep them there. This can draw an entire generation of managers into the business for the wrong reasons, jeopardizing the quality of leadership as well as the children's personal fulfillment and job satisfaction.

Other parents keep pay artificially low to impress upon children the importance of frugality. This can deprive the business of an important asset: a committed, aggressive and highly qualified management and employee team. The company suffers.

Business owners find that using pay as a multipurpose tool to control family members becomes so complex and burdensome, and creates so many distorted expectations, that they eventually regret it.

Pitfall Four: Using Pay to Ease Uncomfortable Emotions. Parents usually want to help their children and may be uncomfortable when one makes less than another. In response, a parent may give a pay raise or make private gifts to the underdog. In other cases, parents are uneasy when cousins from different branches of the family are paid differently. "Why is my kid worth less than his?" a business owner may wonder. Others are guided by their perceptions of a child's needs — as in the case of the Smiths, raising pay when a new grandchild is born, for instance.

Nothing is wrong with a parent expressing support and concern for a child. But entangling emotional issues with pay decisions can engender mistrust and distorted expectations. Because a family business will inevitably wind up paying some family members more than others or individual family members will appear needy from time to time, a systematic, merit-based approach to pay has no substitute.

Pitfall Five: Preserving Secrecy Around All Pay Issues. Popular wisdom holds that to talk about how much you are paid is indiscreet, impolite or just plain wrong. Also, many business owners are reluctant to start compensation planning because they fear others will attack their pay. They want to avoid such questions as, "Why do we do it this way?" and "How much should a CEO be paid?" Even if the questions are not actually asked, the business owner may be self-conscious about those issues and wish the whole subject would go away. Some even keep children's pay secret from their bosses. This can badly demoralize the managers involved, who may legitimately wonder whether their position of authority is a charade.

That doesn't mean communicating about gifts has to be a major issue. Many families simply inform members quietly and discreetly or make a statement during a family meeting. This creates an opportunity for family members to air concerns that, once expressed, can be resolved before they erupt into crises.

Pitfall Six: Confusing Business and Personal Funds. The business owner also may worry about financing a secure, independent retirement but may not want to admit a need to take extra pay out of the business. He or she may see keeping control over compensation as a way to assure that retirement needs are met quietly and discreetly.

Again, there are benefits in informing successors and, ideally, an outside board, about retirement needs. Independence and financial security for the retiring CEO are too important to be swept under the rug. They are fundamental to any sound compensation plan. Without it, the retiree's cash demands are an unpredictable drain on the business. It can make it impossible for successors to plan for and manage those needs in a systematic way. Trying to hide retirement needs only delays the "day of reckoning."

Pitfall Seven: Taking Relationships for Granted. Discussing pay with a subordinate, while always difficult, becomes nearly impossible for many people when the subordinate is also a family member. To avoid it, many business owners assume that family members will trust, respect and be satisfied with their paychecks, just because they are a family member. "I'm her father," they reason. "Of course she knows that I'm going to take good care of her. She'll trust me to be fair, because she's blood." In most family businesses, that means family employees get fewer performance reviews and less education about compensation than other employees.

Taking relationships for granted can be a big mistake. Pay is even *more* sensitive when it involves a family member, and the issue can foster enormous resentment and misunderstanding. Everyone concerned has an opinion about pay, and family members who are not working in the business have a particularly keen interest in the way family employees are paid. These factors make a strong communication and education effort crucial, not only to family harmony but to business success.

Pitfall Eight: Providing Salary Substitutes. Many family businesses err by trying to appease family members dissatisfied with their paychecks with extra titles, status or perks. An example:

When a daughter in one family business asked for more pay, her father struggled with a response. She was doing well, but he didn't want to re-open the subject of pay and didn't really know how to value what she did. So he made her a vice president with no pay raise.

This well-intended effort will probably backfire. As a vice president she will probably feel justified in expecting even more pay in years to come. Like any salary substitute, the vice presidency will merely become evidence supporting her argument for more money. Worse yet, this "title inflation" risks destroying respect within the organization for titles of responsibility. Eventually, they will be taken for granted. Ultimately, the issue is the same: there is no substitute for a sound pay policy consistently applied.

Pitfall Nine: Paying Everyone Too Little — or Too Much. A common practice in family business is to hold down top-management pay as a way of suppressing compensation throughout the organization. Many entrepreneurs view compensation as an expense rather than an investment in developing a valuable resource — skilled and knowledgeable employees. They may even redefine jobs to trim pay, particularly when they hire from outside the business, on the reasoning that they don't want to "coddle" their employees.

These same business owners may boast about spending a little more for a top-of-the-line truck or piece of equipment. But they have a blind spot on the issue of compensation. Rather than structuring pay and incentives in a way that lures highly qualified employees, these family businesses adhere to a feudal concept: pay underlings just enough to keep them coming to work.

Jerry-rigging the pay system in this way can have some major consequences. Though keeping relative pay in line throughout the business is an excellent practice, as discussed later in this booklet, holding it artificially low can harm the self-esteem, loyalty, morale and performance of valued employees. It can foster high turnover until the work force is mediocre at best. A less common tendency among business owners is to pay too much. Some business owners may want to be seen as generous. They don't want their children or other employees to question their pay levels, since talking about compensation is always awkward. Paying people very well increases retention and avoids the hassle of filling in for and replacing people who quit. Hefty paychecks also can be golden handcuffs that bind adult children to the business.

Unfortunately, high pay often leads people to stick around for the wrong reasons, and the long-term costs can be damaging. Not only do family members and other employees develop a distorted perception of their own value, but the big paychecks protect them from the need to continuously develop their potential. Companies that reason this way rarely even let low performers go.

Pitfall Ten: Using Pay to Level Out Ups and Downs in Profit. Entrepreneurs are often sensitive to how they are perceived by offspring or others in the business. The result may be an unconscious tendency to pay too much when the business is doing poorly, and to pay too little when the business is doing well. Though seemingly paradoxical, this pattern meets two personal needs for the entrepreneur. If the business is doing poorly, the owner may worry, "I want the kids to know I've got a great business here and I'm doing a great job running it." So he or she raises pay, bonuses or perks to encourage that point of view. Conversely, when the business is doing well, the entrepreneur may feel less need to prove he or she is a good leader. Then, pay suffers as the entrepreneur plows more money back into the business. Regard for the compensation system suffers too, as employees wrestle with the mixed messages.

Summary

Compensation is second only to succession as a concern in family business owners' minds. The importance of the issue is growing, as more second and third generation heirs enter management of family businesses. Questions about paying family members and others can become increasingly complex and unmanageable as a family business grows and passes from generation to generation. As a result, many business owners are embracing rational, systematic compensation policies aimed at encouraging both professional growth among employees and strategic accomplishment in the business.

The mission of a good compensation plan is to keep everyone involved in the business working for what is best for all. Designing such a plan can force business owners to express their most fundamental goals. A philosophy of compensation that conveys positive values — such as stewardship of assets, personal initiative and teamwork — can have a powerful impact on everyone it touches.

Most business owners build a compensation philosophy on a framework that "pays the job" — rewarding employees based on the market value of their position. Others employ additional "qualitative" criteria that include certain leadership, analytical, communication or other skills required to do the job with in that particular business. Still others choose to pay family members more equally.

Beyond that, larger family businesses may use various combinations of short- and long-term incentives to tie employees' pay to the performance and strategic goals of the business. Pay can be structured to stress other values as well, such as teamwork, the importance of shareholder value, or the value of entrepreneurial initiative. Because compensation planning forces such a fundamental appraisal of the goals of the business, it often leads to other efforts to prepare for the future, including strategic planning and personal financial planning by the business owner.

Business owners should begin early to shape children's attitudes about compensation in the business. Living modestly and "paying the job" from the moment a son or daughter first enters the business can help shape expectations to match future realities. Talking about compensation also is a natural way to help children begin planning careers within the business and preparing for the future structure of family management.

As the family business and the number of shareholders grow, many

59

family businesses adopt more open and professional compensation policies similar to those in public companies. Some bring in a compensation consultant or name an active outside board to help resolve disagreements over pay between shareholders who are active in the business and those who are not. If nonfamily executives assume key roles, many families develop creative means such as "phantom stock" to reward and retain these valuable employees without diluting the family's ownership stake. An outside board, a trusted accountant or a compensation consultant can all provide helpful advice on such complex subjects.

Once a compensation philosophy is established, the business owner must work to build trust in it. The philosophy should be communicated clearly to family members and other employees in individual sessions, executive meetings, staff meetings or family meetings. The message should be conveyed in a way that makes the business owner's priorities clear and stresses the relationship between employee pay and broader strategic goals. These talks can lay the foundation for educating employees about the business, exploring such questions as, "What is profit and what is it used for?" or "What kind of business cycles affect our industry?" Perhaps most important, exceptions to compensation policy should be avoided, at risk of destroying credibility and trust.

Recommended Reading Resources

BOOKS

In Search of Excess: The Overcompensation of American Executives, by Graef S. Crystal, the controversial book that caused the media to scrutinize executive compensation. Published by Norton in 1992.

Compensation And Motivation, by Thomas J. McCoy, (AMACOM, 1992) and *Compensation Handbook* by Rick Milton, (McGraw- Hill, 1991) are two good "textbooks" on general compensation.

SURVEYS

Salary Increase Survey Report, Hewitt Associates, Lincolnshire IL. Telephone 847-295-5000.

National Executive Compensations Survey, The Management Association, Westchester IL. Call 708-344-6400.

MAGAZINES

Forbes magazine's listing of the "200 Best Small Companies in America" (usually in the November issue).

Index

The Authors

Craig E. Aronoff and John L. Ward have long been recognized as leaders in the family business field. Founding principals of the **Family Business Consulting Group**, they work with hundreds of family businesses around the world. Recipients of the Family Firm Institute's Beckhard Award for outstanding contributions to family business practice, they have spoken to family business audiences on every continent. Their books include *Family Business Sourcebook II* and the three-volume series, *The Future of Private Enterprise.*

Craig E. Aronoff, Ph.D., holds the Dinos Eminent Scholar Chair of Private Enterprise and is professor of management at Kennesaw State University (Atlanta). He founded and directs the university's Family Enterprise Center. The center focuses on education and research for family businesses, and its programs have been emulated by more than 100 universities worldwide. In addition to his undergraduate degree from Northwestern University and Masters from the University of Pennsylvania, he holds a Ph.D. in organizational communication from the University of Texas.

John L. Ward, Ph.D., is Clinical Professor of Family Enterprises at Northwestern University's Kellogg Graduate School of Management. He is a regular visiting lecturer at two European business schools. He has also previously been associate dean of Loyola University Chicago's Graduate School of Business, and a senior associate with Strategic Planning Institute (PIMS Program) in Cambridge, Massachusetts. A graduate of Northwestern University (B.A) and Stanford Graduate School of Business (M.B.A. and Ph.D.), his *Keeping the Family Business Healthy* and *Creating Effective Boards for Private Enterprises* are leading books in the family business field.